RUSSIA
the people

Greg Nickles

A Bobbie Kalman Book

The Lands, Peoples, and Cultures Series

 Crabtree Publishing Company

The Lands, Peoples, and Cultures Series

Created by Bobbie Kalman

Coordinating editor
Ellen Rodger

Project development, editing, and design
First Folio Resource Group, Inc.
Pauline Beggs
Tom Dart
Bruce Krever
Kathryn Lane
Debbie Smith

Separations and film
Dot 'n Line Image Inc.

Printer
Worzalla Publishing Company

Consultants
Theodore H. Friedgut; Larissa Kisseleva-van Amsterdam; Bella Kotik-Friedgut; Evgueni Petrusevich, Consulate General, Russian Federation, Montreal; Sergei Ulianitsky; and Paul van Amsterdam

Photographs
B. & C. Alexander/Photo Researchers: cover; Archive Photos: p. 8 (both); Peter Arkell/Impact: p. 9 (top), p. 21 (bottom), p. 29 (bottom); Corbis/Bettmann: p. 6, p. 7 (top right); Corbis/Dean Conger: p. 14 (right), p. 23 (bottom); Corbis/David Cumming, Eye Ubiquitous: p. 25 (right); Corbis/Natalie Fobes: title page, p. 12 (top), p. 20 (bottom), p. 24 (bottom); Corbis/Wolfgang Kaehler: p. 13 (bottom); Corbis/Steve Raymer: p. 15 (top), p. 20 (top), p. 21 (top right), p. 22, p. 23 (top); Corbis/Michael T. Sedam: p. 3; Corbis/Vince Streano: p. 24 (top); Corbis/Keren Su: p. 12 (bottom); Mimi Cotter/International Stock Photo: p. 5 (bottom left), p. 11 (top); Giraudon/Art Resource, NY: p. 7 (left and bottom right); Andy Johnstone/Impact: p. 10 (left),

p. 31 (right); Wolfgang Kaehler: p. 4 (top), p. 5 (top), p. 10 (right), p. 14 (left), p. 16 (both), p. 17 (bottom), p. 19 (both), p. 25 (left), p. 27 (top and middle), p. 31 (left); Material World/Impact: p. 5 (bottom right), p. 26 (top), p. 29 (top); Mark Newman/International Stock Photo: p. 11 (bottom); Reuters/Peter Andrews/Archive Photos: p. 17 (top); Reuters/Viktor Korotayev/Archive Photos: p. 9 (bottom), p. 13 (top), p. 30 (bottom); Reuters/Volodia Smalivkov/Archive Photos: p. 30 (top); Reuters/Vladimir Suvorov/Archive Photos: p. 28 (bottom); Charles Steiner/International Stock Photo: p. 21 (top left); Adam G. Sylvester/Photo Researchers: p. 27 (bottom); Janet Wishnetsky/ Impact: p. 4 (bottom), p. 15 (bottom), p. 18, p. 26 (bottom), p. 28 (top)

Illustrations
David Wysotski, Allure Illustrations: back cover

Cover: A girl from Nenets, in northwest Siberia, harnesses a reindeer to her supply sled.

Title page: Boys show off their harvest from a successful day of wild mushroom picking.

Icon: King and queen chess pieces appear at the top of each section. Chess is very popular in Russia.

Back cover: The Kamchatka brown bear is a symbol of Russia.

Published by
Crabtree Publishing Company

PMB 16A
350 Fifth Avenue
Suite 3308
New York, NY 10118

612 Welland Avenue
St. Catharines, Ontario,
Canada L2M5V6

73 Limewalk
Headington,
Oxford OX3 7AD
United Kingdom

Cataloging in Publication Data
Nickles, Greg, 1969-
    Russia--the people / Greg Nickles.
      p.cm. -- (The lands, peoples, and cultures series)
    Includes index.
    Summary: Describes city and rural life, family customs, traditional dress, food, pastimes, schools, and problems created by the struggling economy in this vast federation.
    ISBN 0-86505-239-5 (RLB) -- ISBN 0-86505-319-0 (pbk.)
    1. Russia (Federation)--Social life and customs--Juvenile literature. [1. Russia (Federation)--Social life and customs.] I. Title. II. Series.
    DK510.32.N53 2000
    947--dc21
                                      LC 99-056058
                                               CIP

Contents

♟ A proud people ♟

Russians are a proud people with a long history. They come from many backgrounds, speak a wide variety of languages, and have diverse **customs** and ways of life.

Many Russians' lives are filled with hardships. Their work is difficult, and they get paid little. Necessities such as food and medicine are expensive compared to their salaries. People also struggle against the country's harsh climate, which is one of the coldest in the world.

Despite the hardships, Russians enjoy life. They love food, games, and sports. They observe many special traditions and celebrations. Most importantly, they spend as much time as possible with their friends and loved ones.

(left) A man from the eastern region of Magadan carefully carves an ivory sculpture.

(below) A girl living in the Caucasus Mountains of Dagestan carries a bundle of hay to feed her family's goats.

Three friends walk to the park where they plan to join in a pick-up game of soccer.

A father pulls his son through a park in St. Petersburg.

A mother comforts her daughter who is worried about starting a new school.

Russia through the ages

Russia's history stretches back many centuries. Throughout this time, powerful leaders brought Russia wealth and glory, but also caused many hardships for the people.

Kievan Rus

About 1700 years ago, tribes of farmers and cattle herders from central Europe moved east. They settled in the present-day countries of Czechoslovakia, Poland, Ukraine, and Romania. These people became known as the East Slavs. For the next five hundred years, they worked as craftspeople, farmers, and traders, building towns and cities on river routes. In 882, a group of Vikings, led by Prince Oleg, took over the East Slavs' land and founded the kingdom of Kievan Rus. The city of Kiev, in present-day Ukraine, was the most powerful city in the land.

Mongol rule

Kievan Rus was independent until the 1200s, when it was conquered by the powerful Mongol **Empire**, to the east. The Mongols were known for their fierce armies of mounted warriors. They were led by Genghis Khan, who conquered China, northern India, and central Asia before turning to Russia in 1222. During the centuries of Mongol rule, the Russians exchanged goods and ideas within the Mongols' empire. Mongol control ended in 1480, when Prince Ivan III, who governed the city of Moscow and the surrounding areas, named himself **czar**, or emperor. Ivan III came to be known as Ivan the Great.

Actors in a 1930s movie recreate a thirteenth-century battle between Russians and northern European invaders.

Rule of the czars

From 1613 onward, all czars came from the powerful Romanov family. The Romanovs ruled for over three hundred years. During this time, they introduced Russia to modern ideas, arts, and architecture from Western Europe. They also fought many bloody wars and built Russia into a huge empire. By the end of the nineteenth century, Russia controlled lands stretching from Eastern Europe west to the Pacific Ocean.

The czars lived in luxury, but they made most Russians into **serfs**. Serfs grew crops for themselves on land that was owned by a landlord. They were forced to work for the landlord without pay and to give him a share of their own harvests. Russia remained a nation of landless peasants, while other countries built important new **industries** such as mines, iron and steelmaking factories, and railroads.

In 1547, Ivan IV, known as Ivan the Terrible, crowned himself czar. In his brutal drive to increase the territories of Russia, he killed thousands of Russians, including his own son.

Peter the Great was czar from 1682 to 1725. He encouraged Russians to adopt many of the customs, fashions, and arts of Western Europe.

Czaritza Catherine the Great ruled from 1762 to 1796. During her reign, she promoted science and the arts, and expanded the Russian Empire.

Russia's last czar, Nicholas II, and his family were taken prisoner and shot by the Communists.

The Soviet Union

By the 1900s, Russians were tired of living under the czars' harsh rule. Hoping to improve people's lives, a **Communist** leader named Vladimir Ilyich Lenin took control. Like other Communists, Lenin believed that the government should own and manage all farms, factories, banks, and other businesses, and set the prices of all goods. Lenin led Russia into a **revolution** and bloody **civil war** that lasted from 1917 to 1921. Then, in 1922, Lenin's Communist government formed the Union of Soviet **Socialist** Republics (U.S.S.R.), or Soviet Union. Russia and fourteen of its neighbors were forced to become part of one state. All people had to follow the laws set by the **Soviet** government in Moscow.

Building a nation

In the following decades, the Soviet government changed the country into a modern industrial nation. In spite of the improved **economy**, life was very difficult for the people. Soviet citizens suffered under a brutal ruler named Joseph Stalin, who was in power from 1929 until his death in 1953. Soviets also fought in World War II (1939–1945), during which 25 million Soviet citizens died.

During his rule, Joseph Stalin terrorized and murdered millions of people whom he considered "enemies of the state."

End of the Soviet Union

After World War II, the U.S.S.R. continued to grow as a world power. Despite the country's successes in rebuilding and improving people's lives, shortages of food, clothing, and other everyday goods were common by the 1980s. Citizens were also frustrated that the government did not allow them to speak freely, travel to other countries, or practice their religion openly.

Mikhail Gorbachev, who became the Soviet leader in 1985, tried to improve daily life. His achievements included *glasnost*, a "new openness" in which more ideas and free speech were allowed, and *perestroika*, a program to improve the economy. His efforts did not satisfy the people, who finally gave up on the Soviet Union in 1991. Russia and the fourteen other **republics** of the U.S.S.R. split away to form their own countries. The Soviet Union ceased to exist. ·

(right) Russians show their support for Boris Yeltsin, the first leader of democratic Russia, in 1991.

(below) A statue of Lenin lies abandoned, pushed over by demonstrators during the collapse of the Soviet Union.

A new Russia

Russia's new government is a **democracy**, with leaders who are elected by the people. The government has encouraged a **free market**, in which ordinary Russians run the country's businesses and set their own prices as they compete for customers. People have begun to enjoy freedom of speech, travel, and religion. Certain parts of the country have not changed as quickly as others, and daily life is still very hard for most people throughout Russia. Prices are high, and many people cannot find good jobs. In spite of these difficulties, everyone hopes that the changes will one day make Russia a better place to live.

♟ Peoples of Russia ♜

There are over 130 **ethnic groups** in Russia. People from each group speak the same language, practice the same religion, and share a common history. The largest group is made up of ethnic Russians. They are **descended** from the East Slavs who inhabited Kievan Rus.

Ethnic Russians

Since the time of the czars, ethnic Russians have held the power in the country. The majority live in the western parts of Russia. Many follow the Russian Orthodox Church, a **denomination** of Christianity. Christianity is based on the teachings of Jesus Christ, who Christians believe is the son of God. Many ethnic Russians, however, do not believe in any religion at all. During Soviet rule, religion was restricted and most young people grew up with very little knowledge of any **faith**.

Boys carrying homemade wooden fishing poles hope to make a big catch in the nearby river.

Ukrainians and Belorussians

Two other ethnic groups, the Ukrainians and Belorussians, are also descended from the East Slavs. During Mongol rule, when most Russian lands were cut off from the rest of the world, the Ukrainians and Belorussians still had contact with empires to the west. Each group developed slightly different languages than the ethnic Russians and separate cultures. Today, most Ukrainians and Belorussians live in the independent countries of Ukraine and Belorussia, but large groups still live in western Russia.

A woman eats a juicy persimmon. This fruit is a favorite Christmas treat in Russia.

Tatars, Bashkirs, and Chuvash

Some of Russia's other large ethnic groups include the Tatars, Bashkirs, and Chuvash. All three groups trace their histories to the ancient Bulgar people and to the Mongols who once ruled Russia. Both the Tatars and Bashkirs follow Islam, a religion based on the teachings of the **prophet** Muhammad. The Chuvash are mostly Christians.

Peoples of the Arctic

Many small ethnic groups survive in the harsh landscape of Russia's far north, including the Inuit, Aleut, Chukchi, and Evenki. Some of these Arctic people live as nomads, while others live in villages built by the government during Soviet times. Arctic peoples follow many beliefs, including the teachings of their own religious leaders, called **shamans**. Many also worship the spirits that they believe live in nature.

A man holds his well-bundled child.

A Siberian girl plays with her pet dog. Her family is nomadic. They live in large tents and move from place to place, hunting reindeer for their hides and meat.

♛ Russian families ♛

Family is an important part of Russian life.
Family members rely on one another for love
and friendship, food, entertainment, and a
warm home to go to in the cold weather.

*(top) A mother helps her child balance on his
brand new scooter in the Siberian town of Sireniki.*

*(below) Three children and a live-in **babushka**
make this Russian family a large one.*

Raising a family

In Soviet times, mothers received a special title,
"Mother Hero," if they had more than four
children. Today, large families are still respected,
but it is expensive to raise more than one or two
children. It is also difficult to find an apartment
or house that is roomy enough — especially in
the city. The cost of homes is so high that grown
children and their new husbands or wives must
often live with their parents for several years
after they are married.

Center of the family

Children are the center of a
Russian family. Parents spoil
them with whatever treats
they can afford, and make
enormous **sacrifices** to
ensure they have the best
possible clothes, toys, and
food. Raising children well
is considered so important
that strangers sometimes
scold parents in public if
their child misbehaves or is
poorly dressed.

What is in a name?

Russian children have three names. The first is their given name, chosen by their parents. The middle name is their father's first name plus a special ending. For example, if a father's name is Pavel, his daughter's middle name will be Pavlovna. His son's will be Pavlovich. The last name is the family name, at the end of which girls add an "a." For example, if a father's last name is Sakharov, his daughter's last name will be Sakharova.

Hard at work

Both men and women in a family work to help pay for housing, groceries, and basic appliances such as refrigerators and stoves. Even after the work day is done, many adults take on extra jobs to earn a little more money for the family. Sometimes young children also help by working in their spare time.

(right) **Babushka** *ventures out on a snowy day to a street-side market and finds a good deal on eggs for her family.*

(below) A man spends an afternoon with his granddaughter by a river in Irkutsk.

Babushka lends a hand

Many families invite the *babushka*, or grandmother, to live with them after her husband dies. This custom dates back to village times, when several generations used to live together in one home. Today, while parents are away at work, the *babushka* looks after the young children, cleans the house, does the grocery shopping, and cooks. Sometimes *babushkas* also take on odd jobs, such as selling home-cooked goods, scrubbing floors, or shoveling snow, to help support the family.

♚ Family customs ♚

Family life in Russia is filled with many customs and celebrations. Some are old folk traditions or religious events. Others are more modern customs, introduced during or after Soviet times.

Swaddling

Traditionally, mothers used to **swaddle**, or wrap, young babies in cloth. Swaddling prevented babies from injuring themselves and was believed to help their bones grow straight. Children were swaddled each day, from the time they were born until they were about three months old. Today, swaddling is usually practiced in only the most remote parts of the country, where people still follow the old traditions.

Birthdays and name days

As in North America, many Russian children celebrate their birthday with a party. Members of the Russian Orthodox Church often celebrate their name day as well. In the Church, each day of the year belongs to a different saint, or holy person. When a new person is welcomed into the Church, he or she receives a saint's name. That saint's day of the year becomes the person's name day. People mark their name day by going to church and having a dinner and party.

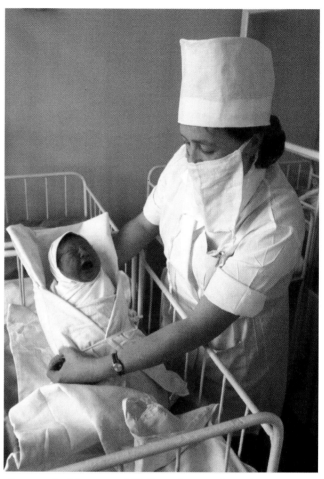

A nurse holds a swaddled newborn who will be unwrapped only to eat, bathe, and play.

Honored guests

Russian families love having guests. They follow many customs to make sure their guests' stay is a welcome one. When guests arrive, the host goes out the door to greet them, or brings them immediately into the home. It is considered bad luck to greet guests on the **threshold**. Traditionally, important guests were welcomed with a dish of salt placed on top of a loaf of bread and presented on a fine cloth. The guest was expected to taste the bread and salt, which were symbols of health and happiness. Today, this custom is usually followed only to welcome high-ranking officials from Russia and other countries.

Women in traditional costume offer a welcoming of bread and salt.

Old and new weddings

The Soviet government tried to replace religious weddings with simple ceremonies performed by a local official. Since the end of the Soviet era, more and more people are choosing to be married in a religious ceremony.

During a Russian Orthodox wedding, the bride and groom hold candles and exchange rings three times. The priest performs other **rituals** such as offering the couple a sip of holy wine and leading them around the church three times.

Wedding feasts

After the ceremony, family and friends greet the newlyweds at their reception dinner. Guests cry out "Gorko!" during the meal, meaning "The food is bitter!" The couple must kiss to make the food sweet again. As the bride and groom kiss, guests count out loud. It is said that the higher the number at the end of the kiss, the more the newlyweds love each other.

A Russian Orthodox priest blesses crowns held over the heads of five couples getting married at the same time.

Guests at an outdoor wedding sing and dance in celebration.

♟ City life ♟

Most Russians live in towns and cities. Although Russian cities are very overcrowded, people continue to move there in the hope of finding work. There are also plenty of things to do in cities: eat in a restaurant, go to the theater, visit an art gallery, or stroll in a park.

City homes

Almost all city dwellers live in square, cement apartment buildings, which can be very crowded. An apartment usually has one or two bedrooms, an eat-in kitchen, a bathroom, and a living room that may be converted at night for sleeping.

(right) Many cities are filled with cement apartment buildings constructed by the former Soviet government.

(below) A trolley trundles down a street in Vladivostok, a port city on Russia's east coast.

Short supply

For many years, there were shortages of fresh vegetables and fruit in the cities. Today, these shortages are rare, except sometimes during the winter. Food tends to be expensive, especially meat. Some city dwellers are able to get meat much cheaper from relatives in the countryside who raise **livestock**.

A woman, who has finally made it to the front of a long line at a butcher shop, looks expectantly for another counter person.

The waiting game

In the days of shortages, good shoppers were always on the lookout for unexpected supplies. They rarely left home without a shopping bag in case they came across a great deal. If they did, they immediately phoned friends and relatives to notify them. Then, the shoppers stood in line, holding a place for all those they called. Standing in line was both an art and a profession. Some *babushkas* would add to their **pensions** by getting paid to stand in line for someone else.

Escaping to the *dacha*

Many city families are lucky enough to own a small wooden country cottage, called a *dacha*. *Dachas* may have electricity, but there is usually no running water. Families visit their *dacha* on the weekends to escape the bustle of city life. They also come to tend their garden, where they grow food to take back to the city.

At their **dacha,** *families grow potatoes, tomatoes, cabbage, cucumbers, and other vegetables that can be pickled or preserved for the long winter.*

Living in the country

About one-quarter of Russia's population lives in the vast countryside. Many people work for large, government-run farms or on one of the many small, private farms that have been started in recent years. Life in the country is much different than in the city. The day's pace is more relaxed, the countryside is less crowded, and people often eat better because they raise their own food.

Country homes

Country homes are a mix of the new and old. In some villages, people live in boxy houses made of concrete. Although small, these homes have basic utilities. Most country homes, however, are cozy houses made of wood or brick. They have double window panes and padded doors to keep cold winds from blowing in during the winter. Most of these homes have electricity. The toilet, well, and pump are sometimes located outside. A large wood-burning stove in the middle of the home provides heat and a place to cook.

Country hardships

Country life can be very difficult because villages and farms are far apart and isolated. There are often no paved roads, so walking, cycling, or riding in a horse-drawn wagon or sled are the most common means of transportation. Schools are often small and lack good textbooks, supplies, and teachers. Health clinics in most villages have only basic medical supplies, and getting to the closest hospital is often difficult. Many people rely on their own home remedies, using plants to cure common illnesses.

On the farm

Men, women, and children all help out on Russian farms. They tend the crops and raise livestock such as cattle, hogs, and sheep. Then, they take their produce into town to sell at the "bazaar," which might be a large market place or just a line of vendors along the side of the road. This produce is very popular with city people because of its freshness and good quality.

In mountainous Dagestan, in southwestern Russia, village houses are often built right into the hillside.

(above) In Siberia, children help plant, tend, and harvest the crops because the growing season is short.

(below) In Siberia, families paint the outside of their houses in bright colors. These colors add cheer to the stark, snowy landscape during the long winters.

Going to school

A good education is important to Russians. In the past, the country's education system trained many skilled scientists and taught almost all Russians to read and write. Today, teachers hope to offer their students as good an education, but are worried that their schools may not have enough money to function.

A student at the Repin Academy of Art, in St. Petersburg, considers his half-finished painting.

Russian children exercise outside during gym class.

Busy days

Russian children go to classes five or six days a week between September and May. Young children start school at about 8:30 a.m. and finish at 12:30 p.m., while older children finish classes at 2:30 p.m. Schools stay open after classes so that children can play sports. In the evenings, students do the piles of homework that their teachers give them.

School years

Many young children attend preschool, although children do not have to go to school until they are seven years old. During their first four years at school, students learn mathematics, physical education, and history. Then, they begin to study science, literature, geography, and a foreign language. After grade nine, some students go to a **vocational** high school to learn a trade such as farming or mechanics. Other students specialize in a particular subject, such as science or mathematics. They hope to enter a university or college for a career in engineering, medicine, teaching, or another field.

Students try out new programs in the school's computer lab.

Special talents

At an early age, many students with outstanding skills in mathematics, sports, languages, ballet, or other arts attend special schools. In the morning, they study the same subjects as students in other schools. In the afternoon, they have classes that develop their special talents.

New texts

Russia had a strong education system in Soviet times, but students were discouraged from asking questions. As well, textbooks did not tell the truth about Russia and the world. Some teachers knew the texts were so filled with false information that, after Soviet rule ended, they did not use textbooks at all! Today, Russian schools encourage discussion, and accurate textbooks teach children about their own culture and about cultures around the world.

Making do

Many Russian schools have little money. They must make do with few supplies, old equipment, and buildings that lack heat or indoor plumbing. Some parents send their children to expensive new private or religious schools, which were not allowed in Soviet times. These modern schools have up-to-date equipment, and often have better teachers than the free public schools.

(above) Students gather around a sculpture during a field trip to the Summer Gardens in St. Petersburg.

A teacher helps her students during social studies class.

A special day

Katya shivers as she looks out the window at the snowy yard in front of her family's apartment building. Katya is excited because her uncle Boris is coming to visit from Siberia.

"Finish your breakfast or you'll be late," her mother warns. Katya quickly eats the last of her bread and stewed fruit. Then, she goes to the living room and folds her bed neatly back into the sofa.

Soon, with her homework in her backpack, Katya is ready for school. Katya's mother is also leaving. She is going to a cleaning job. Katya remembers when her mother worked full-time at the chemical plant, but it closed. "Jobs are hard to find nowadays," her mother had said. "We're lucky your father has a good job, even if he has to travel across town."

Outside, Katya waves good-bye to her mother and walks past the blocks of concrete apartment buildings in her neighborhood.

On her way to school, she meets Sasha, from her grade seven class. Suddenly, they are pelted with snowballs! They turn to see Sasha's little brother, Dmitri, packing together more snow.

"Stop it or I'll tell Father. You won't be able to watch cartoons tonight!" Sasha scolds. Dmitri sticks out his tongue and runs ahead to school, laughing. "Sometimes I wish I were an only child like you, Katya," Sasha sighs. "Sometimes I wish you were, too!" Katya jokes, wiping the snow off her coat and backpack.

In the morning, Katya presents her science project on rocks and minerals. Later, in the lunchroom, she eats her meal of fish soup and bread. Then, it is time for English class. Katya enjoys the class, but the school's old ceiling begins to leak water onto her desk. When classes end, Katya races to the school gym to practice her gymnastics routine. She hopes to improve her routine on the parallel bars before the local competition next week.

Katya catches up to Sasha on the way to school.

When Katya returns home, she is delighted to hear that her mother bought a surprise treat for Uncle Boris's visit. They both work quickly to prepare the table, and Katya remembers to plug in the **samovar** to boil hot water for the tea. Soon, Katya's father returns from work. He is very tired but too excited about his brother's visit to take a nap.

Before long, there is a knock on the door. Katya's father welcomes Boris and his fiancée, Valentina, with many hugs and kisses. Boris has brought flowers for Katya's mother and a small gift for Katya — a **brooch** with a beautiful green stone. "I made it for you from one of the rocks I mined," he says. Katya is thrilled and gives her uncle a hug.

As everyone sits down to dinner, Katya's mother brings out her surprise — a tin of black **caviar**, the family's favorite treat. As everyone eats, Boris and Valentina talk about their new home and their wedding plans. Katya is having so much fun that she wishes this special day will never end.

(above) Katya's mother busies herself in the crowded kitchen, preparing dinner.

(below) Boris and Valentina stand in front of their new home in Siberia.

♟ Food ♟

Russians enjoy many kinds of hearty food. Favorite dishes include a beet soup called *borscht*; *shchi*, a cabbage soup; *kasha*, which is cooked oats, buckwheat, or another grain; and *pirozhki*, which are fried or baked rolls filled with meat, eggs, rice, or vegetables.

Bread with every meal

Bread is so important to the Russian diet that people coined the saying, "Without bread, it is not a meal!" There are countless kinds of bread, many of them dark, heavy, and very tasty. Russians buy bread with care, studying its color and weight, and tapping it with a flat spoon to test if it is properly baked.

The samovar

A large, elegant urn called a samovar sits on the dinner table of almost every Russian home. It is a portable container that boils water for tea. The finest samovars are tall, made of silver, and decorated with many patterns. Older samovars were built to burn pinecones and charcoal as fuel. Today, most samovars are powered by electricity.

(above) Finely crafted samovars are cherished objects that are often passed on to younger family members.

(below) A baker sets out bread pans filled with raised dough before popping them in the oven.

Special occasions

Whenever they can, Russians love to have a special dinner with guests. These meals begin with *zakuski*, which are appetizers such as cold cuts, smoked fish, pickled vegetables, and caviar, a salty delicacy made from fish eggs. Salads, soup, and a meat dish follow. Dinner might also include *blini*, thin pancakes with jam, sour cream, or meat wrapped inside.

A boy chooses a jar of pickled vegetables from the pantry where his family stored it months before.

"Potato" treats

With the help of an adult, you can make "potato treats," a tasty dessert that looks like small potatoes. You will need:

750 mL (3 cups) bread crumbs
75 mL ($\frac{1}{4}$ cup) white sugar
170 mL ($\frac{2}{3}$ cup) unsalted butter or margarine
a dash of vanilla extract
125 mL ($\frac{1}{2}$ cup) milk
15 mL (1 tbsp) icing sugar
15 mL (1 tbsp) cocoa powder
a cookie sheet
a small pot
two mixing bowls

Spread the bread crumbs on the cookie sheet. Roast them in the oven until slightly golden. Mix the crumbs in a bowl with the white sugar, butter, and vanilla extract. In a pot on the stove, warm the milk slightly. Then, mix it gradually into the bowl, being careful not to make the mixture too gooey — it should become a thick dough.

To make the insides of your "potatoes," roll the dough, then cut off small pieces and shape them into potato-sized balls. For the "skin," mix the cocoa and icing sugar in a bowl. Roll your potatoes in the mixture until well-coated. Chill before serving.

A cook chops dill to season a picnic of smoked fish, bread, cheese, caviar, and red currants.

♛ What to wear ♛

Russian day-to-day clothing is very similar to the clothes that people wear in Western Europe or North America: pants, shirts, blouses, skirts, jeans, and sweaters. Russians take very good care of their clothes because they are expensive. Most people cannot afford a large wardrobe. They usually have just a few outfits for the summer and winter seasons.

Bundle up!

In a country where winter can last for more than half the year, people must bundle up in very heavy, warm clothes. Wool is used to make scarves, sweaters, mittens, socks, and underclothes. Fur is also used because it is very warm and inexpensive — there are many fur-bearing animals in Russia's vast forests.

A young village girl wears warm gloves, heavy boots, and a **shapka** *to protect her from the cold.*

These men, who live in the chilly heights of the Caucasus Mountains in Dagestan, wear sheepskin coats and fur hats.

From top to bottom

One of the most common pieces of winter clothing that women, men, and children wear is the large *shapka* hat. A *shapka* is made of soft fur and has large, floppy flaps. These flaps can be tied up or left down to cover a person's forehead and ears. Russians also wear sturdy winter boots. Leather and rubber footwear are common, as are warm *valenki* — boots of thick felt, a fabric made of pressed wool.

(above) Russian children in a folk group wear beautifully embroidered dresses and shirts.

Traditional clothing

Today, traditional clothes are worn only on special occasions such as at festivals or folk dancing performances. These clothes look like the clothes that Russian peasants wore more than a century ago. They were often homemade and beautifully embroidered with colorful stitching. Women wore a simple blouse with a skirt or sleeveless dress called a *sarafan*. Men had trousers and linen shirts. Everyone wore embroidered hats, and often warm sheepskin vests or overcoats. In winter, *valenki* warmed their feet, but in summer, cool shoes woven from tree bark were common.

(above) On special occasions, young women in Ulan Ude, near Mongolia, wear the traditional costume of their people.

(below) Many older women wear large colorful scarves on their heads called, in North America, **babushkas** *after Russian grandmothers.*

♟ Sports and pastimes ♟

Russians have many fun ways to pass the time. Sometimes they stay in with their families, watching television or playing games or music. When not at home, they enjoy doing everything from cheering on their world-class gymnasts in competition to having wild snowball fights.

Winter fun

Cold weather brings the chance to play all sorts of winter sports, including hockey. Russia has some of the world's best professional hockey players, and fans regularly pack arenas to watch them play. Russians also enjoy ice fishing, skating, tobogganing, and cross-country skiing.

Summer sports

During Russia's short summers, millions of fans watch or play soccer. Track-and-field sports, hiking, and fishing are also popular. During the peak of the hot weather, pools, beaches, and river banks are packed with swimmers.

These men belong to a "Walrus Club," a group of swimmers who take a special New Year's dip when the waters are freezing cold!

During the summer, families and friends gather for picnics, music, and games.

In the *banya*

Each week, many Russians look forward to their trip to the *banya*, a large steam bath. Russians believe that the hot steam is good for their health. Each bath can hold many people, so friends meet there to talk. It is customary to buy a branch of birchwood at the door to the *banya*. While inside, bathers gently hit the branch against their skin, hoping to cleanse their pores and improve their blood circulation. Following their hot steam bath, people take a quick dip in freezing water or sometimes jump into the snow before they dry off and get dressed.

Checkmate!

Russians are passionate about chess, the most popular and respected game in the country. Millions of fans, from children to senior citizens, play regularly. Crowds gather in halls or parks to watch matches and to comment as their friends compete. During Soviet times, the government promoted chess as an activity in which everyone could participate and which would develop people's minds. Today, young people start to play chess during their first years at school. Thousands of Russian children play the game so well that they have been awarded the high rank of chess master.

Two chess players study the board intently, planning their next moves.

Hockey players and skaters spend hours on rinks, frozen rivers and lakes, or any other place where there is a large patch of ice.

♛ Looking to the future ♛

An elderly man sells home-grown cucumbers at a roadside stand, hoping to earn a bit of extra money.

Russians are living through a time of many changes. The switch from the old Communist system to one based on democracy and a free market has brought new opportunities, but many hardships as well.

Unemployment and poverty

One of the worst problems that Russians face is unemployment. In Soviet times, everyone had a job. Today, millions of people are out of work because companies that were too outdated to make a profit in the free market were forced to close. The free market has also driven up prices, making it harder for everyone to afford the basic necessities of life.

(top) A crowd cheers and raises a Russian flag to show its support for the democratic government.

Living together

Today, Russia's government allows the country's many ethnic groups to celebrate their cultures. Most of these groups live peacefully, but some are unhappy. In the mid-1990s and again in the late 1990s, war broke out between the Chechens and the Russian government. This group of people, from a region of Russia called Chechnya, wanted the right to form their own country, independent from Russia. More fighting may break out in other areas if other groups make the same demands.

Questions for the future

Russians disagree on how to solve their country's problems. Many people dislike the democratic government and its free-market strategy. They believe it has made their troubles much worse than in Soviet times, and want to return to the ways of the past. Many others disagree, saying that Russia needs more time to grow into a **stable** and wealthy democracy. No one knows for sure what changes are in store for Russians, their government, and their way of life; however, most people feel that change should continue.

(above) Two young girls speed around together on a tricycle.

(right) A father and son walk together in a Moscow park.

Glossary

brooch A decorative pin worn on clothing

caviar The salty-tasting eggs of sturgeon, a type of fish

civil war A war between different groups of people or areas within a country

Communist A person who believes in an economic system where the country's natural resources, businesses, and industry are owned and controlled by the government

custom Something that a group of people has done for so long that it becomes an important part of their way of life

czar The title given to Russian emperors

democracy A form of government in which representatives are elected to make decisions for society

denomination An organized religious group within a faith

descended Having roots to a certain family or group

economy The way a country organizes and manages its businesses, industry, and money

empire A group of countries or territories having the same ruler

ethnic group A group of people who share a common race, language, heritage, or religion

faith A religion

free market Trade without high taxes or strict government control

industry The making of things using factories

livestock Farm animals

pension A sum of money paid regularly by a country or business to a person who has retired from work

prophet A person who is believed to speak on behalf of God

republic A country that is not led by a king or queen

revolution An uprising or war against a government

ritual A formal act performed in a specific situation

sacrifice The act of giving up important or valued things for the sake of something or someone else

samovar A metal urn with a tap; used for boiling water for tea

serf Up to the 19th century, a person who had to live and work on land owned by a lord

shaman A person believed to have access to good and evil spirits

Socialist Following an economic system where the country's natural resources, businesses, industry, and politics are controlled by the whole community

Soviet Having to do with, or a citizen of, the Union of Soviet Socialist Republics (U.S.S.R.), which existed from 1922 to 1991

stable steady, unlikely to change suddenly

threshold A doorway, or a piece of stone or wood below a door

vocational Leading to a trade or occupation

Index

1 2 3 4 5 6 7 8 9 0 Printed in the USA 5 4 3 2 1 0